REJOICE!

(Originally published as *Christmas Inspirations*)

FULTON J. SHEEN

IMAGE BOOKS
A Division of Doubleday & Company, Inc.
Garden City, New York
1984

Image Books edition published September 1984
by special arrangement with Anthony C. Sparacino, Publisher Communications, Inc.
Originally published as *Christmas Inspirations*.

Nihil Obstat: Daniel V. Flynn, J.C.D., Censor Librorum
Imprimatur   Terence J. Cooke, D.D., V.G.
Archdiocese of New York, September 9, 1966

Library of Congress Cataloging in Publication Data
Sheen, Fulton J. (Fulton John), 1895–1979.
Rejoice!
1. Christmas—Meditations.   I. Title.
BV45.S42   1984   242'.33

REJOICE!

Divinity Is Always Where You Least Expect to Find It

There was no room in the inn, but there was room in the stable. The inn is the gathering place of public opinion, the focal point of the world's moods, the rendezvous of the worldly, the rallying place of the popular and the successful. But the stable is a place for the outcasts, the ignored, the forgotten. The world might have expected the Son of God to be born — if He were to be born at all — in an inn. A stable would be the last place in the world where one would have looked for Him. *Divinity is always where one least expects to find It.*

No worldly mind would ever have suspected that He Who could make the sun warm the earth would one day have need of an ox and an ass to warm Him with their breath; that He Who, in the language of Scriptures, could stop the turning about of Arcturus would have His birthplace dictated by an imperial census; that He Who clothed the fields with grass would Himself be naked; that He from Whose Hands came planets and worlds would one day have tiny arms that were not long enough to touch the huge heads of the cattle; that the Feet which trod the everlasting hills would one day be too weak to walk; that the Eternal Word would be dumb; that Omnipotence would be wrapped in swaddling clothes; that Salvation would lie in a manger; that the bird which built the nest would be hatched therein — no one would ever have suspected that God coming to this earth would ever be so helpless. And that is precisely why so many miss Him. *Divinity is always where one least expects to find It.*

If the artist is at home in his studio because the paintings are the creation of his own mind; if the gardener is at home among his vines because he planted them; and if the father is at home among his children because they are his own, then surely, argues the world, He Who made the world should be at home in it. He should come into it as an artist into his studio, and as a father into his home; but, for· the Creator to come among His creatures and be ignored by them; for God to come among His own and not be received by His own; for God to be homeless at home — that could only mean one thing to the worldly minded: the Babe could not have been God at all. And that is just why they missed Him. *Divinity is always where one least expects to find It.*

Transparency by Francis G. Mayer, N.Y.C.

"I Bring You Tidings of Great Joy"

This message of the Angels was given to the shepherds and they were sore afraid. Nature fears in the Presence of God. The Angel told them to "fear not," for man is not to fear when God unveils the splendor of His majesty. Man is like a harp unstrung; most of the music of his soul's strings is discordant as they wail with sorrow and anxiety. But the Son of David, the great Harpist comes down to move His Fingers among the strings of our soul, and to make them as beautiful as the melody of the angel-song. This is why the shepherds were not to fear.

There was fear first among the shepherds, then joy. First there is the fast, and then there is the feast; one must have the shadow to show the light. If there had been no rebellion on the part of man, there would have been no freedom with Christ. The Christmas message is first the fast, then the feast. The world has first the feast, and then the headache. The joy that Christmas brought comes from release from anxiety, fear, dread, all of which are the pallbearers of our guilt. Once that Child was born, God would now look upon humanity and remember that His Son is a Man like to us. As often in a war a feud is ended when the opposing parties intermarry, so there is no more war between God and man because God has entered into nuptials with humanity.

Shepherds

A comedian said that he had applied for unemployment insurance: he was a shepherd. This has humor because in our cosmopolitan civilization there are not many shepherds. But the rest of the world is full of them and the most memorable of them all were the shepherds in the hills of Bethlehem at Christmas. It was said that they raised the lambs that were sacrificed in the temple. If this be so, they came to see the true Lamb of God.

Messages came to many in the Old Testament who were shepherds. Moses received his credentials as the ambassador of the Most High and the lawgiver of a nation while feeding the flocks of Jethro. Abraham was a shepherd; so was David. Ezechiel, a prophet centuries before, had foretold, "Behold I will raise you a shepherd," and St. Peter calls Christ the "Chief Shepherd."

What interests us is that God called the shepherds while they were still at work doing their duty. An Angel appeared to Gideon when he threshed wheat by a winepress. Saul, looking for the lost donkeys of his father, found a kingdom and himself. Elisha was plowing when Elijah passed the mantle of prophecy to him. Amos was with the herdsmen of Tekoa when he saw God's judgment upon Tyre.

The best place in all the world to be for higher summons is at a post of duty. Nowhere else are great temporal and spiritual blessings to be sought. When the Lord has a great gift or message to give to one of His children, He sends it to the place where the child ought to be found. It matters very little what we are doing; what does matter is that we are doing our duty. Sometimes the most humble occupations prepare for the greatest vocations. Society is built up from below. The roof is more dependent upon the foundation than the foundation upon the roof. Nearly all the movements which have changed the thinking and the course of the world have been upward, not downward. Civilization is a debtor to lowly cradles, to unknown mothers who are denied places in an inn, and to humble shepherds working in the night.

Why We Are Lovable

There are only two philosophies of life: one, the pagan, the other, the Judaic-Christian. In all pagan religions man tries to climb to God. In the Judaic-Christian tradition God descends to man: first by revelation to the prophets for the Jews, and finally in the flesh in the Person of Jesus Christ, the Son of God. "God, Who gave to our forefathers many different glimpses of the truth in the words of the prophets, has now given us the Truth in the Son."

In religions such as Buddhism, Confucianism, Hinduism, and the like, man is the wooer and God the wooed; man the seeker and God the found. In the Judaic-Christian tradition, the role of man to God is that of mirror to light, the echo to the voice. "God so loved the world that He gave His only begotten Son so that everyone who believes in Him may have eternal life." Love originates not in our showing it to God, but in His showing His Love for us. God loved us first. God's love for us is not affirmed because we seek Him or reach out to Him, and He responds to us. God does not love us because we are lovely or lovable; His love exists not on account of our character, but on account of His. Our highest experience is *responsive,* not initiative. And it is only because we are loved by Him that we are lovable.

It is true that as men mount in knowledge and in virtue, it *seems* as if God begins then to love them; this is only because they are now, for the first time, sensitive to His love, or because they removed the barriers that kept the love of God from shining upon them. A man who is blind from birth, having had an operation on his eyes which restored his sight, might think that the sun was just beginning to shine in the heavens and the flowers just beginning to bloom. But all of these things existed since the beginning, although his eyes were not in the condition to see them. Every child at the age of six or seven begins to be conscious of his mother's love, but the mother bestowed love on her child before the child was born; the maternal solicitude and love existed before the child was conscious of affection. It is only because we are loved by God that we are lovable!

What Can We Love?

If we were naturally good, there would have been no need of Christ coming to earth to make us good. "Those who are well have no need of a physician." If all were right with the world, God would have stayed in His Heaven. His Presence in the crib in Bethlehem is a witness not to our progress, but to our misery. If we had a totally satisfying love without hate, or nausea, or fed-upness, would we still feel unloved?

Christmas is the season for exchanging gifts with friends; so Our Lord came to exchange gifts. He says to us, as only a good God could say: "You give Me your humanity and I will give you My Divinity; you give Me your time and I will give you My Eternity; you give Me your weary body and I will give you My Redemption; you give Me your broken heart and I will give you My Love; you give Me your nothingness and I will give you My All."

The human heart has many loves flung at it, but none of them can wholly satisfy. Love of humanity is impossible, because there is no such thing as humanity—there are only men and women. The religion of progress is impossible, because progress means nothing unless we know where we are progressing. Even a theory about love leaves us cold, because man can never fall in love with a syllogism. It has even been suggested that we should love the cosmos, but the cosmos is too big and too bulky. *"Nature, poor stepdame, cannot slake my thirst."*

Man has never loved and will never love anything he cannot get his arms around. That is why the Immense God became a Babe in order that we might encircle Him in our arms.

Seville Cathedral

This Will Be the Sign: A Babe

Andrea da Firenze

If we just sat down and thought out how we would expect God to come to this earth, we would generally agree that it would be with trumpeting splendor, flashes of light, thunders, and in the midst of them all full panoplied the glory of Divinity. But this is because we come in our pride, judge power by greatness. Because human pride had to be broken, the angels were given a "sign": a "Babe wrapped in swaddling clothes lying in a manger."

Since He came to save us from our guilt, and not to manifest His Power—that will come at the end of the world—He was bearing the only cross a Babe can bear: poverty and the limiting swaddling bands of our humanity. To be our Savior, our Redeemer, our Emmanuel, He must enflesh Himself in the very race He came to save, and not with one man or a few men, but with humanity. He must go down to the very rock from which we are hewn and put on our nature—not in its decorated, ornamental form—but as it is in the humblest and weakest. If He had come in any other form, He would have misled us concerning the purpose of His coming, namely, "to save us from our sins." The poor now could not say He does not know what it is to be homeless. The lowly could now not say He does not know what it is to be despised. The ignorant could not say He does not know what it is to be childlike. He took on every form of humiliation of which our frustrated humanity was capable, in order to show men how to struggle through the darkness into the light. To some it may be an unreasonable tax upon faith to see a Babe in a manger, but it is actually a sign of God's condescension to human weakness. If He had come in power and glory, it would not have been a sign, just as it would be no sign or proof that the sun was in the heavens to see it shining at midday. If there is to be a sign, it must be contrary to what we would expect. But the sun that is eclipsed is a sign. And so is the God wrapped in swaddling clothes.

The Three Ages of the Babe

Some years ago W. Gascoyne Cecil recorded his observations on the way art depicts the Three Wise Men. He observed that they were generally represented as of different ages. One was old, one middle-aged, and one young. The tradition has it that this belief came from the lips of the great traveler, Marco Polo, who, when he went to Persia, tried to find out all he could about the Wise Men. Finally coming to a little town, he found there a devotion to the Three Kings who had followed a star to worship a great Being born in the West, and their ages were very different.

As Gascoyne Cecil tells the story, when they came to the stable at Bethlehem, "they went in one at a time. First went in the old man, and instead of finding what he had expected, he found an Old Man who talked with him. He was then followed by the middle-aged man. He in his turn was met by a Teacher of his own years who spoke with him. When the young man entered in, he in his turn found a young Prophet.

"The three met together outside the stable and marvelled—how was it that all three had gone in to worship this Being Who was just born, and they had not found a Child, but three Men of different ages? The old man had found the Old, the middle-aged the Middle-Aged, and the young the Young. Taking their gifts they go in all together, and are amazed to discover that the Prophet is then a Babe of twelve days old! Each sees separately in Christ the reflection of his own condition. The old man sees the old, the middle-aged the middle-aged, and the young the young. But when they go all in together, they see Christ as He is. We shall find in Christ the answer to all our needs, and all the periods of our life."

"Word Made Flesh": What Does It Mean?

This is the way Scripture describes Christmas — "The Word was made Flesh and dwelt amongst us." Is there anything in our experience that can make us understand it? Suppose we take the word "dog." A boy in a family often uses the word "dog," and even talks about it so much that he almost begins to live in its companionship. The parents catch the enthusiasm and since they have shared in his desires, a dog is ordered. The bell rings at the front door. Everyone rushes to the hall, and there is a "dog"! Up until then "dog" was only a word. It is no longer a word. It is a "word made flesh." It dwells in the family and they behold its joys.

Christmas is the enfleshment of the eternal Person of God; the beginning in time of the Human Nature of Him Who is without beginning or end. When I go to a blackboard and write the word "Love," the idea of love does not begin to exist at that moment; it already had existence in my mind for years. What actually happens is that "love is made chalk and dwells on the blackboard." So too, when Christ took upon Himself a manhood from the womb of His Mother Mary the "eternal Word was made Flesh and dwelt amongst us."

That is why Jesus only once in His Life said that He was born, but He immediately added that He "came into the world." This is the way He always expressed His eternal Person — as "coming into the world," because He had eternal preexistence. He Who created the world is born in the world; He Who made time is measured by it.

When, therefore, He moved about the earth, He was God teaching through a human mouth, God healing through human touch, God suffering in a human body. And all this to make us Divine as He made Himself human.

Love Without Lust

The Virgin conceived Our Lord without the lust of the flesh, so she brought forth Him in joy without the labor of the flesh. As a bee draws honey from the flower without offending it, as Eve was taken out of the side of Adam without any grief to him, so now in remaking the human race, the new Adam, Christ, is taken from the new Eve, Mary, without any sorrow to her. As our minds beget a thought without in any way destroying the mind, so Mary begot the Word of God without in herself in any way affecting her virginity. In flesh-love the ecstasy is first in the body, and then indirectly in the soul. In the Spirit-love it was Mary's soul that was first ravished, and then, not by human love, but by God. The love of God so inflamed her heart, her body, her soul, that when Jesus was born the whole world could truly say of Him, "This is a Child of love." As Chesterton put it:

> That Christ from this created purity
> Came forth your sterile appetites to scorn.
> Lo! In her house Life without lust was born
> So in your house lust without Life shall die.

Samuel H. Kress Collection

HOW OLD WAS JOSEPH?

Why has Christian art always pictured Joseph as aged? Was it in order to better safeguard the Virginity of Mary? Somehow or other the assumption has crept into art that senility is a better protector of virginity than adolescence. Painting thus unconsciously made Joseph a spouse chaste and pure by age rather than by virtue. But this is like assuming that the best way to show that a man would never steal is to picture him without hands; it also forgets that old men can have unlawful desires as well as young men, for it was the old men in the garden who tempted Susanna. But more than that, to make Joseph out as old portrays for us a man who had little vital energy left, rather than one who, having it, kept it in chains for God's sake for His holy purpose. To make Joseph appear pure only because his flesh had aged is like glorifying a mountain stream that is dried.

Is it not more reasonable to believe that the Babe would have preferred for a foster father someone who had made a sacrifice rather than someone who was forced to it? If Our Lord did not disdain to give His Mother a young man, John, at the foot of the Cross as her protector, then why should He have given her an old man at the Crib? A woman's love always determines the way a man loves; she is the silent educator of his virile powers. Since Mary is the real "Virginizer" of young men as well as women, the greatest inspiration of Christian purity, should she not logically have begun by inspiring and "Virginizing" the first man whom she probably had met—Joseph? It is not by diminishing his power to love but by elevating it that she would have her first conquest, and in her spouse, the man who was a *man* and not a mere senile watchman.

15

Abba, Father

"God is dead!" said Nietzsche in the last century, and in this our day, lesser lights proclaim it. Some only mean that it is difficult to comprehend, explain, and describe the nature of God—which indeed is true. But Christmas changed that by reminding us that God is Father. As Paul put it: "When the fullness of time was come, God sent forth His Son made of a woman, made under the law, to redeem men that were under the law, that we might receive the adoption of sons." (Gal. 4:4)

In earthly adoption, foster parents are unable to communicate to the adopted child their nature. In Divine adoption, which is a prolongation of the Incarnation, we become partakers of the Divine nature. That is why as Christ called God His Father, so we too may call Him Father, because we are, as St. Peter explained, "Partakers of the Divine Nature."

This will have great importance on the Last Day, when we are judged. Just as a mother knows her own children because they share her nature, so Christ, looking into our souls, will recognize if we share His nature, and that we have the same Heavenly Father. He will then say to us: "Come, ye blessed of My Father, into the Kingdom prepared for you from all eternity." If He looks at those who lack this resemblance, He will say, "I know you not." And it is a terrible thing not to be known by God!

Once we share the nature of the Babe in the crib, then there begins to be a communication of life and reciprocity of love. It is a love in which the Father bestows and the child receives; because it is derived, it is kindred, and because it is kindred it enfolds itself in likeness to the Father that gave it. Between the Father's heart and the Son's heart there passes a blessed interchange, a quick correspondence, an answering love flashing backward and forward like the lightning that touches the earth and rises from it again.

One Christmas the English poet Francis Thompson took a little child into a church in order that they might look at the image of the Christ Child in the crib. The poet then put into the mouth of the child the questions that a child might have asked the Child, namely, how it feels for the God of Heaven to live as a Child on this poor earth of ours.

"Little Jesus, wast Thou shy
Once, and just so small as I?
And what did it feel like to be
Out of Heaven and just like me?
Didst Thou sometimes think of there,
And ask where all the angels were?
I should think that I would cry
For my house all made of sky;
I would look about the air,
And wonder where my angels were;
And at waking 'twould distress me —
Not an angel there to dress me!
Hadst Thou ever any toys,
Like us little girls and boys?
And didst Thou play in Heaven with all
The angels that were not too tall,
With stars for marbles? Did the things
Play *Can you see me?* through their wings?
And did Thy Mother let Thee spoil
Thy robes, with playing on *our* soil?
How nice to have them always new
In Heaven, because 'twas quite clean blue!

Didst Thou kneel at night to pray,
And didst Thou join Thy hands, this way?
And did they tire sometimes, being young,
And make the prayer seem very long?
And dost Thou like it best, that we
Should join our hands to pray to Thee?

I used to think, before I knew,
The prayer not said unless we do.
And did Thy Mother at the night
Kiss Thee, and fold the clothes in right?
And didst Thou feel quite good in bed,
Kissed and sweet, and Thy prayers said?

Sacred Heart Messenger

Thou canst not have forgotten all
That it feels like to be small:
And Thou knowst I cannot pray
To Thee in my father's way —
When Thou wast so little, say
Couldst Thou talk Thy Father's way? —

So, a little Child, come down
And hear a child's tongue like Thy own;
Take me by the hand and walk,
And listen to my baby-talk.
To Thy Father show my prayer
(He will look, Thou art so fair),
And say: "O Father, I, Thy Son,
Bring the prayer of a little one."

And He will smile, that children's tongue
Has not changed since Thou wast young!

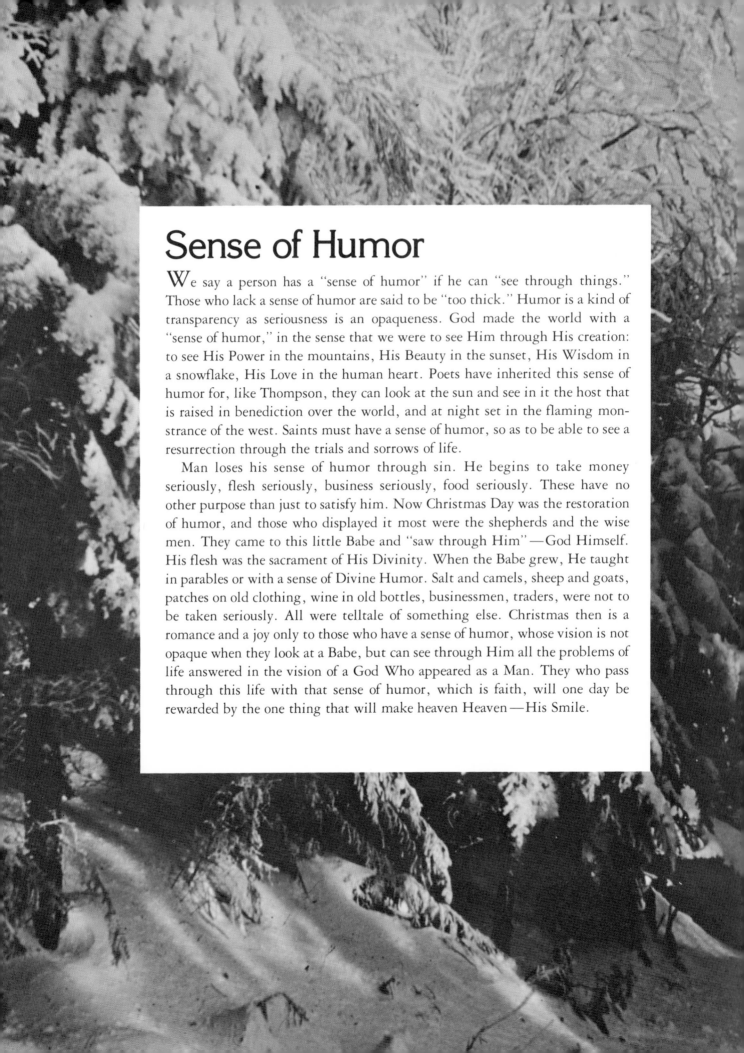

Sense of Humor

We say a person has a "sense of humor" if he can "see through things." Those who lack a sense of humor are said to be "too thick." Humor is a kind of transparency as seriousness is an opaqueness. God made the world with a "sense of humor," in the sense that we were to see Him through His creation: to see His Power in the mountains, His Beauty in the sunset, His Wisdom in a snowflake, His Love in the human heart. Poets have inherited this sense of humor for, like Thompson, they can look at the sun and see in it the host that is raised in benediction over the world, and at night set in the flaming monstrance of the west. Saints must have a sense of humor, so as to be able to see a resurrection through the trials and sorrows of life.

Man loses his sense of humor through sin. He begins to take money seriously, flesh seriously, business seriously, food seriously. These have no other purpose than just to satisfy him. Now Christmas Day was the restoration of humor, and those who displayed it most were the shepherds and the wise men. They came to this little Babe and "saw through Him"—God Himself. His flesh was the sacrament of His Divinity. When the Babe grew, He taught in parables or with a sense of Divine Humor. Salt and camels, sheep and goats, patches on old clothing, wine in old bottles, businessmen, traders, were not to be taken seriously. All were telltale of something else. Christmas then is a romance and a joy only to those who have a sense of humor, whose vision is not opaque when they look at a Babe, but can see through Him all the problems of life answered in the vision of a God Who appeared as a Man. They who pass through this life with that sense of humor, which is faith, will one day be rewarded by the one thing that will make heaven Heaven—His Smile.

What Is a Man The Higher Evolution

From the evolutionary point of view it is perhaps true that the body of man is a push from below, but Christmas teaches that man is also a gift from above. He is not only of the earth earthly, he is also of the heaven heavenly; not only a risen beast but a fallen angel. He is therefore not supposed to act like a beast because he came from one, but to act Divinely because made to God's own image and likeness.

Man is not only a little biochemical entity of flesh and blood not more than six feet tall, apt to be killed by a microbe, standing self-centered in such a universe as this, acknowledging no future and still hoping that blind cosmic forces of space and time will sweep him on until he becomes lost in the bursting of the great cosmic bubble. Rather, Christmas shows that though he has much in common with lower creation, it is possible for him to respond to the gift which God brought to earth on Christmas.

Looking at Him, image of what we were meant to be, we see not only our actual ignorance, but our possible wisdom; not only our actual sinfulness, but our possible saintliness; not just our actual humanity, but our possible sharing in His Life. Then, by an act of self-distrust, which is the highest kind of self-assertion, we enroll ourselves under no less a Person than the Son of God made man, saying, "I am thine O God, help me whom Thou hast made."

Old Print

We Live Below
Our Possibilities

Most of us live below the level of our receptivity. We could be more educated than we are; more healthy than we are; and more musical than we are. These failures are often due to a want of opportunity, or a want of will and resoluteness. But granted even these, there is a limit to what man can do by his own powers. Our philosophy today is obsessed with the idea that man can lift himself by his own bootstraps.

Christmas brings the message that we can be *receptive* of a gift. As the Manhood that God took from Mary was Divinized, so too our human nature can also be Divinized to some degree by making Bethlehem contemporary, and by submitting ourselves to the open Hands of God. But we are always afraid that if we give Him our finger He will take our hand, not realizing that we are only surrendering the spark in order to get the Flame.

Our human nature is measured not by what it can impart primarily, but by what it can receive. The ox at the Crib could receive but little outside the sweetness of the grass and the coolness of the water. A dog can receive more than an ox, because he looks at his master as an inferior looks at his superior in whom one discovers a greatness. In a way, the dog finds "deity" in his master, for from him he learns both law and love.

If we look upon Christmas as something that happened twenty centuries ago, then we forget our receptiveness to the Divine Life and Truth and Love which was brought to this earth and which is still available. If we open the windows, sun and wind will play through our dwelling. It was no wonder that that Babe when He grew to a Man said to the women at the well, "If thou didst know the gift of God." Never until God dwelt in the flesh could any man know what our poor weak flesh could become.

Adoration of the Magi (Hieronymus Bosch), Metropolitan Museum of Art, Kennedy Fund, 1912

He the Sun; She the Moon

Bartolommeo Morelli

One cannot go to a statue of a mother holding a babe, hack away the mother, and expect to have the babe. Touch her and you spoil him. She is the window through which our humanity first catches a glimpse of Divinity on earth; perhaps she is more like a magnifying glass that intensifies our love of her Son and makes our prayers more bright and burning. He is the sun, she is the moon. On dark nights we are grateful for the moon; when we see it shining, we know there must be a sun. So in this dark night of the world when men turn their backs on Him Who is the Light of the world, we look to Mary to guide our feet while we await the sunrise.

WHAT IS PEACE?

The message of the Angels of Christmas was "on earth peace." What is peace? Peace is the tranquillity of order. It is not just tranquillity alone, for thieves can be tranquil in the possession of their spoils. Order or justice is the due subordination of parts to whole, of body to soul, and of man to God. Without order there can be no true tranquillity, which is peace.

The Christmas gift of peace was the uncoiling of the links of a triple chain which first unites men with God, then man with himself, and then man with his fellowman.

WHY WE MISS PEACE

One reason why we do not find peace is that we want to be saved but not from our vices, or because we want to be saved but at not too great a cost, or because we want to be saved in our way and not God's way. We miss peace because in each and every one of us there is a little secret garden which we keep locked. It contains the one thing we will not give up to have true peace of soul; it may be alcohol, it may be an unholy alliance. The Christmas secret of peace is giving this secret garden and our whole human nature to God, as Mary gave Christ His human nature. Christmas reminds us that the reason we are not as happy as saints is because we do not wish to be saints.

EMMANUEL

About eight centuries before Christ was born, the prophet had foretold that He would be born of a Virgin and would be called Emmanuel, which means "God with us." The sun is so bright that we do not see all of the colors contained in it unless its rays are shot through a prism. God's Divinity is too great for us; it was necessary that it be shot through the prism of a human nature, so that we might begin to comprehend God's love for us. This is the meaning of "Emmanuel"— "God with us." He Who is born without a mother in heaven is born without a father on earth. He Who made His Mother is born of His Mother. He Who made all flesh is born of the flesh. The Bird that built the nest of the universe is hatched therein. Maker of the sun, under the sun; Molder of the earth, on the earth; ineffably Wise, little Infant; filling the world, lying in a manger; ruling the stars, suckling a breast; the mirth of heaven weeps, God becomes Man; the Creator, a Creature; the Rich becomes poor; Divinity, incarnate; Majesty, subjugated; Liberty, captive; Eternity, time; Master is servant; Truth, accused; Judge is judged; Justice, condemned; Lord, scourged; Power, bound with ropes; King, crowned with thorns; Salvation, wounded; Life, dead; Union of unions, three mysterious unions in One—Divinity and humanity, virginity and fecundity, faith and the heart of a man. And though we shall live on through eternity, eternity will not be long enough for us to understand the mystery of the Child Who was a Father, and the Mother who was a child.

Giving Presents

"And when we give one another our Christmas presents in His Name, let us remember that he has given us the sun, the moon and the stars, the earth with its forests, and mountains, and oceans and all that lives and moves upon them. He has given us all green things and everything that blossoms and bears fruit—and all that we quarrel about and all that we have refused. And to save us from our own foolishness and from all our sins He came down to earth and gave Himself. *Venite Adoremus Dominum.*" (Sigrid Undset, *Christmas and Twelfth Night,* Longmans Green, 1932)

What Can I Give?

There is only one thing in the world that is really our own—and that is our will. Everything else we have received and can be taken away from us. Our will is ours for all eternity. That is why the most precious gift that one can give another is his will. He Who came to this earth on Christmas Day did not say "If you know Me you will do My will" but "If you do My will you will know Me."

Christina Rossetti has expressed this well in her little poem:

What can I give Him,
Poor as I am?
If I were a shepherd
I would bring a lamb,
If I were a wise man,
I would do my part—
Yet what can I give Him,
Give Him my heart.

(*Collected Poems,* Macmillan)

Come and Worship the Child

The Russian peasantry for centuries had propagated a curious tradition. It is about an old woman, the Baboushka, who was at work in her house when the Wise Men came from the East and passed on their way to Bethlehem to find the Child. "Come with us," they said. "We have seen His star in the East, and we go to worship Him."

"I will come, but not now. I have much housework to do, and when that is finished, I will follow and find Him." But her work was never done. And the Three Kings had passed on their way across the desert and the star shone no more in the darkened heavens.

Baboushka never saw the Christ Child, but she is still living and still searching for Him. And though she did not find Him, out of love for Him, she takes care of all His children. It is she who in Russian homes is believed to fill all the stockings and dress the tree on Christmas morn. The children are awakened with the cry, "Behold, the Baboushka!" And they jump up, hoping to see her before she vanishes out of the window. She is like the Santa Claus of the Western world. The tradition has it that she believes that in each poor little child whom she warms and feeds, she may find the Christ Child Whom she neglected long ago. But she is not doomed to disappointment, for the Divine Child said, "He who receives one of these little ones in My name, receives Me."

24

They bring the Christ Child presents they have made or grown, hunted or sold. They perform or offer simple gestures of thoughtfulness.

Santons may have inspired St. Francis to re-create the scene of Jesus' birth at Greccio in 1223, usually given credit for ushering in the tradition of Christmas crèches. Some think that Lady Pica, Francis' mother, may have brought an early Nativity set with her from Beaucaire (or Tarascon) in France when she married Lombard merchant Pietro and moved to Assisi.

Provençal santon figures are delightfully anachronistic: They do not portray people of Jesus' day, but rather typical characters of an 18th- or 19th-century village in France.

> Wonderful anachronisms abound in santon scenes. Provencal villagers of the 18th and 19th century come to give the Holy Family gifts of their labor. St. Francis, whose re-creation of Jesus' birth in 1223 started the crèche tradition, often joins them.

Origins of the Tradition

The santon tradition began with small figures of wood or wax or clay that were traded around the Mediterranean, possibly originating in Naples (which went on to develop its *presepios*). Santons existed in the 13th century, in the provinces of the Midi and along the banks of the Rhône River. The French kept

DECEMBER 2004

Museum of Art, Bequest of Maitland F. Griggs, 1943

newspapers as so many years
...rist. The spiritual birth also
...for it creates a crisis in the
...ing a new set of values, new
...and new impulses in life.
...gonism. The birth at Bethle-
...tility of Herod, and the birth
...uls awakens the hostility of
...and its impulses, which are
...he promptings of the spirit.
...birth that St. Paul insisted
...om prison to his beloved peo-
...asking that Christ may dwell
...aith and that they be rooted
...ve. This is the second Bethle-
...l relationship of the individ-
...d Christ, its Supreme Lover.

who deny the existence of

Luc-Olivier Merson

Are We All Innkeepers?

There are many who know well the first Bethlehem, but have no experience whatever of the joys of the second. The difference between the two is the difference between the innkeeper of Bethlehem, and Mary; between Herod and the shepherds. One can know all about Christ and still not have His birth in the soul. Herod knew all of the prophecies and was not particularly surprised when he heard that Christ was born, but his reaction was persecution.

The reason the story of the innkeeper of Bethlehem holds such an important place in the Christmas story is because it is relived in those who refuse the inn of their souls in the second Bethlehem. The innkeeper had reasons for his conduct identical to those who refuse Christ's rebirth in souls. That innkeeper may have turned away the Incarnate God because He was not known, or because he was very busy with his clients who were pouring into the city for the census. He may also have had an economic reason; namely, Mary should have controlled the birth in some way and not have brought a child into the world in such poverty. Furthermore, the appearance of the Mother and her luggage may have indicated to this man of worldly standards that they were of no great importance.

There is not a person in the world who does not become at some moment of his life the innkeeper of Bethlehem. The decision that he takes depends upon the attitude in his heart toward Divinity. The Divine Visitor may not be given a reception, but He has created a responsibility. Perhaps the principal reason of the innkeeper was that the presence of that pregnant woman and newborn child crying in the night might drive other guests away. That is precisely what Christ's second Bethlehem always does. It drives away other guests of the heart, such as pride, lust, avarice, hatred, selfishness, greed. These guests find welcome in most hearts and are the most respectable guests to some.

Then too, maybe the innkeeper thought it would not be remunerative to accept the Mother and Child. They would not be "paying" guests. It is very likely that the hotel rates went up considerably because of the grave need in housing. Then to be faced with someone who could not pay was intolerable to the profit motive. It is this, as well as love of pleasure, which keeps out the Divine Guest, namely, the love of gain. It is an old cry, ringing through the centuries: *"No room, no room, no room."*

The Infinity of Littleness

How can souls find God? It is a psychological fact that it is only by being little do we ever discover anything big. This law raised to the spiritual level tells us how we can find the immense God, namely, by having the spirit of little children.

In the physical order, have you ever noticed that to a child everything seems big? His father is bigger than any other man in the world, and his uncle, who is standing near the window, is taller than the great oak tree down in the valley. Every child loves the story of Jack and the beanstalk, because to him every beanstalk towers to the sky. As a matter of fact, beanstalks do not scrape the stars, but to a little child they do, because a child is so small that in relationship to himself everything is big—even the beanstalk. It is only when the child grows big that the beanstalk becomes small. It is only by being little that we ever discover how big it is.

There is a close relation between physical littleness, which is childhood, and mental littleness, which is humility. We cannot always be children, but we can always have the vision of children, which is another way of saying we can be humble. In the spiritual order the law remains the same: if man is ever to discover anything big, he must always be making himself little. If he magnifies his ego to the infinite, he will discover nothing, because there is nothing bigger than the infinite. But if he reduces his ego to zero, then he will discover everything big—for there is nothing smaller than himself. How then can man discover God at Christmastime? By making himself little he will discover that something big; by being humble he will find the infinite God in the form of a Child.

Christmas Is Not for "Nice" People

The Name that was given to God Who became Man was Jesus, which means "Savior," Savior from our sins. Christmas is not for "nice" people; it is for "nasty" people. "Nice" people think they are good and need no Savior. "Nasty" people come to Him because they are convertible, aware of their own imperfections and deep sense of needing to be cleansed. Their emptiness is not meaningless, like that of a Grand Canyon, but rather like the emptiness of the manger that can be filled. They have a hunger and thirst for something not of themselves, and so they look to the Lord in the manger, Who is very fond of "nasty" people.

One of the charges against Him was that He ate with sinners; the lost sheep was put upon the shoulders of the Good Shepherd and the ninety-nine were left in the field. The lost coin was found and made an occasion for rejoicing, but there was no party or celebration for the other nine. The Savior takes a child on His knees and says that he will enter the Kingdom of Heaven before the university professor. Because the Lord preferred "nasty" people to the "nice" people, it is very likely that if we could look up into Heaven, we should see some sights that would scandalize us. We would say, "Well, how did that woman get there" or "How did he get in. I knew him when..."

There will be many in Heaven whom we never expected to see there. The greatest surprise of all is that we will be there. God would have been Infinite Goodness if He had never made the world, but unless nasty persons had existed He never could have shown His Mercy toward us, and it is likely that He would never have become Man.

Transparency by Francis G. Mayer, N.Y.C.   29

Modernizing Christmas

What doth it profit a man if Christ is born in Bethlehem a thousand times and yet is not also born in his heart? Christ is the die, and we are the coins which are to be stamped with His Image. He brought a new Life to this world to which we may become incorporated. A rose has no right to say there is no higher life than it, nor an elephant a right to say there is no life above it. The whole universe is tending upward. Chemicals do not enter plants unless the plant life comes down to them to take them up into it. Animals descend to plants and incorporate their life into themselves, as man, going down to the lower creatures, incorporates chemical, plant, and animal life into a superior being.

God came down to this earth in order that He might take each and every one of us up to Himself; but He does not force us. As He asked Mary to freely give Him a human nature, so He asks each and every one of us to give Him our human nature. That is how Christmas becomes a reality in the twentieth century.

Suppose there was a universal plague and millions were dying from its infection. A scientist discovered the remedy and offered to make it available to everyone who would come to him. The tragedy of not prolonging Christmas is the tragedy of not receiving the injection of Divine Life that will liberate us from the infection of our evil.

God became Man in order that He might understand our woes, that He might be a Brother at our side, that we might confide to Him our secrets and confess to Him our sins. What a tragedy that so few Christmas-ize this event. How a few moments given to the thought of Him will smooth a ruffle, elevate a depressed feeling, purify a wrong passion. It was wonderful, marvelous, for God to come to this earth, but the marvel that makes us happy is our coming to Him.

The Kind of Jesus Screwtape Recommends

One of the best spiritual books written in our time flowed from the pen of C. S. Lewis and was entitled *The Screwtape Letters*. It was made up of imaginary correspondence between the old uncle devil in hell, and his young nephew devil on earth. One finds the deepest spirituality in reverse, knowing that the truth is just the opposite of what Screwtape recommends. On the subject of Christmas, in one of the letters we read: "My dear Wormwood, through this girl and her disgusting family the patient is now getting to know more Christians every day and very intelligent Christians too. For a long time it will be quite impossible to *remove* spirituality from her life. Very well then; we must *corrupt* it. No doubt you have often practiced transforming yourself into an angel of light as a parade ground exercise. Now is the time to do it in the face of the Enemy (which is God). The World and the Flesh have failed us; a third power remains. And success of this third kind is the most glorious of all. A spoiled saint, a pharisee, an inquisitor, or a magician, makes better sport in hell than a mere common tyrant or debauchee.

"In the last generation we promoted the construction of such a 'historical Jesus' on liberal and humanitarian lines; we are now putting forth a new 'historical Jesus' on Marxian, catastrophic and revolutionary lines. The advantage of these constructions, which we intend to change every thirty years or so, are manifold. In the first place, they all tend to direct men's devotions to something which does not exist, for each 'historical Jesus' is unhistorical...He has to be a 'great man' in the modern sense of the word—one standing at the terminus of some centrifugal and unbalanced line of thought—a crank vending a panacea. We thus distract men's minds from Who He is and what He did. We first make Him solely a teacher."

Your affectionate uncle Screwtape

Transparency by Francis G. Mayer, N.Y.C.

Three Modern Wise Men

I remember reading an essay that G. K. Chesterton wrote about the Three Wise Men—modernized Wise Men. They came to the great city of Peace which they deeply yearned to enter. They knew there were certain conditions of passing into that blessed Bethlehem. The first brought gold—cold and yellow—which buys most of the pleasures of earth. The second brought not frankincense but the modern science of scent, chemistry, with its power of drugging the natural consciousness, controlling the soil of the earth and the surplus population. The third brought myrrh, which symbolized death; it was a fissioned atom which could turn any city which opposed peace into a Hiroshima of destruction.

They met Joseph at the gate of the palace of Peace. Joseph examined their gifts and refused them entrance. They asked, "What could we possibly need yet to assure peace other than that which buys affluence, controls nature and blacks out the enemies of peace." Joseph whispered in the ear of one what he had forgotten. He whispered in the ears of the other two and they went away sad. They had forgotten the Child.

The "Fallout"

Once upon a time, men lived in fear. They were afraid of war—not so much one on earth or land or sea, but a war against what was evil in their own hearts. The war dreaded was not nuclear, but moral; it was not a threat of what might be destroyed on the outside, but of what might be changed within.

is still light that is feared, but not the Light of God, but a flame ignited by men.

The "fallout" which terrorizes is the tiniest thing in the universe—an atom. Governments, publicists, commentators urge citizens and neighbors to bore like moles into the bowels of the earth; some even urge using violence to resist an intruder.

Into what strange cycle has light taken us! We drove ... Light into a cave—and not a Light we ... One that made us. Now we crawl into ... awe of a light our own hands have ...

... any connection between our lighted ... the Light of the world? We believe

... as man ceases to fear God, he begins to ... fellowman. As soon as the conscience no ... whispers that Someone is looking and we ... to right the wrong, then it begins to ... terror from the neighbor. The true fear ... not servile, but filial, not the dread of a ... ster, but a reverence lest we displease ... whom we love and Who loves us; such is ... devoted son has for his father. But when ... ed to fear God, he feared being killed by ... wman. A guilty conscience imagines ... and frightful troubles which never bother ... with an easy conscience. It is very likely ... hysteria of fear about what our neighbor ... to us is in relation to the state of our con-... The more hidden, repressed, or even ... ilt we have, the more we live in fear.

... roblem then is not only to protect our-... inst others, but how to protect ourselves ... urselves. It is not because they are anti-... we have to fear; it is because we are ... God and the Christian virtues to pass ... lives.

... oner did the angels appear to the shep-... Bethlehem and the glory of God shone ... out them, than they were sore afraid. ... frightened them. But the angels said ... "Fear not." And why "Fear not?" ... "Savior is born"—not a teacher, not a social reformer, not an ethical leader. Fear not, because redemption from sin is available. The Christmas tree is the cross; the gift hanging on it is the Savior Who died that we might live. Christmas never seems to change; it is ever the problem of Light, a cave, and a "fallout."

THE TWENTIETH-CENTURY CAVE

Now, in this twentieth century, the cave has once more come into its own. The refugees are no longer on the earth; they seek shelter under it. It

33

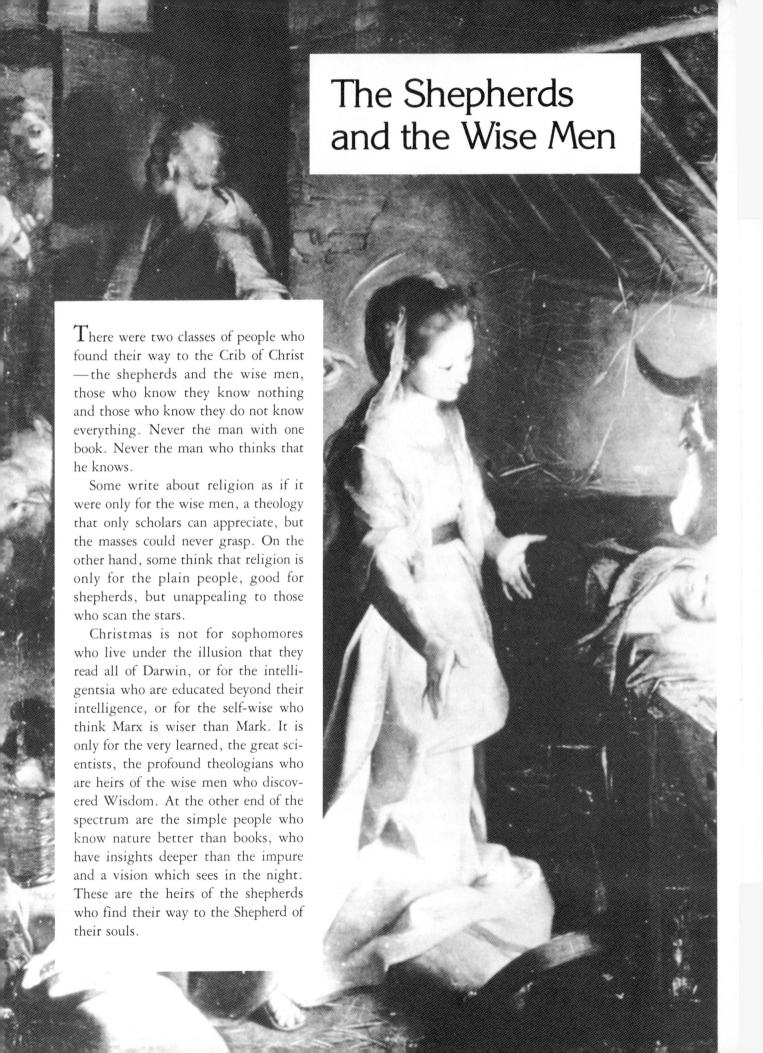

The Shepherds and the Wise Men

There were two classes of people who found their way to the Crib of Christ —the shepherds and the wise men, those who know they know nothing and those who know they do not know everything. Never the man with one book. Never the man who thinks that he knows.

Some write about religion as if it were only for the wise men, a theology that only scholars can appreciate, but the masses could never grasp. On the other hand, some think that religion is only for the plain people, good for shepherds, but unappealing to those who scan the stars.

Christmas is not for sophomores who live under the illusion that they read all of Darwin, or for the intelligentsia who are educated beyond their intelligence, or for the self-wise who think Marx is wiser than Mark. It is only for the very learned, the great scientists, the profound theologians who are heirs of the wise men who discovered Wisdom. At the other end of the spectrum are the simple people who know nature better than books, who have insights deeper than the impure and a vision which sees in the night. These are the heirs of the shepherds who find their way to the Shepherd of their souls.

The Absence of God

We may be living in an age in which we feel more the Absence of God than the Presence of God. We have denied the existence of Bread, but we still hunger; we deny the existence of Wine, but we still thirst. As Thomas à Kempis put it, "If I cannot see Thee present I will mourn Thee absent, for this is also a proof of love."

The loneliness of those who miss the Babe is greatest in those who once had faith and loved Him. Imagine two men marrying two old shrews. One of them was married before to a beautiful young wife who died; the other man was never married before. Which of the two suffers the more? Evidently the one who had the greater love. There is no emptiness in any human heart comparable to the loss of the faith in all that the Incarnation of Christ means: God coming to man that man might be Godlike. As Alice Meynell put it:

He's but conjectured in man's happiness,
Suspected in man's tears,
Or lurks beyond the long, discouraged guess,
Grown fainter through the years

But absent—absent now? Ah what is this
Near as in a child-birth bed,
Laid on our sorrowful hearts,
Close to a kiss? A homeless, childish head.

(*Poems* by Alice Meynell, Charles Scribner's Sons)

New York *Sunday News*—Coloroto Magazine, St. Joseph's R.C. Church Choir

Bethlehem

The little town of Bethlehem is taken from two Hebrew words which mean "House of Bread." He Who called Himself "the Living Bread descended from Heaven" was born in the "House of Bread" and was laid in the place of food, the manger. The first temptation Christ had in the beginning of His public life was to become a bread King, and to win men by supplying them with food. On one occasion when they attempted to make Him King after multiplying the bread, He fled into the mountains. Rome once rang with the cry "Bread and circuses." But the Bread that was brought forth at Bethlehem was an entirely different kind: "Not by bread alone does man live."

The body has its bread. Shall not the soul have its food too? Those who have nourished themselves solely on the bread of the stomach and ignored the Bread of the soul have cried out with some of the bitter disappointment of Lord Chesterfield: "I have seen the silly rounds of business and pleasure, and have done with them all. I have enjoyed all the pleasures of the world and consequently know their futility, and do not regret their loss. Their real value is very low; but those who have not experienced them always over-rate them. For myself, I by no means desire to repeat the nauseous dose."

How a Proud Man Visits the Crib

If a proud man full of sophomoric knowledge entered the stable of Bethlehem, would he ever discover the immense God in that Child? The chances are that he would not. Being so big in his own conceit, he would deny that there is anything bigger than himself: being wise in his own conceit, he would admit nothing wiser than himself; he is so big intellectually that to him everything else is little. To him, that Babe, wrapped in swaddling clothes could not really be a King, for who ever heard of a King on a throne of straw? How could Eternal Wisdom be dumb? He smiles at the credulity of shepherds who believe in angels, at the ignorance of the wise men who believe in the Providential guiding of a star. He lifts his eyebrows at the Virgin Mary, vaguely remembering an Egyptian legend about Arishna. He condescends a glance at Joseph, the man of rags, to whom the innkeeper rightly denied entrance.

"Unless you become as little children," that Babe will say when He grows up; the terrible, frightening, shattering secret of Christmas is that our egotism and pride must be smashed before new light can come in. To enter a cave one must stoop, and the stoop is surrender to littleness. Once one does that, one discovers he is not in a cave at all, but in a new universe, where Wisdom reigns.

The Paradise of Creation

Almighty God never launches a great work without exceeding preparation. The two greatest works of God are the Creation of the first man, Adam, and the Incarnation of the Son of God, the new Adam, Jesus Christ. But neither Creation nor Re-creation happened without the making of a long vestibule for the mansion of each.

God did not make man on the very first day, but deferred it until He had labored for six days in ornamenting the universe. First, by the fiat of His Will, Omnipotence moved and said to nothingness, "Be"; and lo and behold, spheres fell into their orbits passing one another in beautiful harmony without ever a hitch or a halt. Then came the living things: the herbs bearing fruit as unconscious tribute to fecundity and generation; the trees with their leafy arms outstretched all day in prayer; and the flowers opening the chalice of their perfumes to their Creator. With labor that was never exhausting, God then caused to

evolve the sensitive creatures to roam about, either in the watery palaces or on wings to fly through trackless space, or else as unwinged to roam the fields in search of what was needed for their body and blood. But all of this beauty, which has inspired the song of poets and the tracings of artists, was not in the Divine Mind sufficiently beautiful for the creature whom God would make the lord and master of the universe. He would do one thing more: He would set apart as a choice garden a small portion of His creation, and beautify it with four rivers flowing through lands rich with gold and onyx. When finally that Eden was made beautiful, as only God knows how to make things beautiful, He then breathed into the masterpiece of His creation—man, and in that paradise of pleasure was celebrated the first nuptials of humanity—the union of flesh and flesh of the first man and woman, Adam and Eve.

THE PARADISE OF THE INCARNATION

Now if God so prepared a Paradise for His first great work, which was man, it was even more fitting that before sending His Son to redeem the world, He should prepare for Him a Paradise of the Incarnation. For over thousands of years He prepared it by symbols and prophecies. In the language of types, He prepared human minds for some understanding of what this new Paradise would be. The burning bush of Moses inundated with the glory of God, while conserving in the midst of its flame the freshness of its verdure and the perfume of its flowers, was a symbol of a new Paradise, conserving in the honor of its maternity the very perfume of virginity. The rod of Aaron flourishing in the solitude of the temple, while isolated from the world by silence and retreat, was a symbol of that Paradise which, in a place of retirement and isolation from the world, would engender the very flower of the human race. The Ark of alliance, where the tables of the law were conserved, was a symbol of the new Paradise in which the Law, in the Person of Christ, would take up His very residence.

But prophets and symbols were a too distant preparation. God would labor still more on His Paradise. He would make a Paradise not overrun with weeds and thistles, but blooming with every flower of virtue; a Paradise at the portals of which sin had never knocked, nor against the gates of which infidelity would ever dare to storm; a Paradise from which would flow not four rivers through lands rich with gold and onyx, but four oceans of grace to the four corners of the world; a Paradise destined to bring forth the Tree of Life and, therefore, full of life and grace itself; a Paradise in which was to be tabernacled Purity Itself, and therefore one immaculately pure; a Paradise so beautiful and sublime that the Heavenly Father would not have to blush in sending His Son into it. That Paradise of the Incarnation to be gardened by the new Adam, that flesh-girt Paradise in which there were to be celebrated the nuptials, not of man and woman, but of humanity and Divinity, is our beloved Mary, Mother of Our Lord and Savior, Jesus Christ.

OUR THOUGHTS BEFORE THE CHRISTMAS PARADISE

As we gather about the crib of Bethlehem, we feel that we are in the presence of a new Paradise of Beauty and Love and Innocence, and the name of that Paradise is Mary. God labored for six days and produced Eden for the first Adam; now He labored anew, and produced the new Eden, Mary, for the new Adam, Christ. And if we could have been there in that stable on that first Christmas night, we might have seen that Paradise of the Incarnation, but we should not be able to recollect whether her face was beautiful or not, nor should we be able to recall any of her features, for what would have impressed us, and made us forget all else, would have been the lovely, sinless soul that shone through her eyes like two celestial suns, that spoke in her mouth which only breathed in prayer, the soul that was heard in her voice, which was like the hushed song of the angels. If we could have stood before that Paradise, we would have less peered at it as into it, for what would have impressed us would not have been any external quality, though such would have been ravishing, but rather the qualities of her soul—her simplicity, innocence, humility, and above all, her purity. So completely would all these qualities have possessed our soul, like so much divine music, that our first thought would have been, "Oh! So beautiful," and our second thought would have been, "Oh! What hateful creatures we are."

Pietro Saporetti

His Mother Is the Key

Our Lord had only a foster-father, but He had a real mother. It was she who gave to Him His human life—gave Him Hands with which to bless children; Feet with which to go in search of stray sheep; Eyes with which to weep over dead friends and a corrupt civilization; and a Body with which He might suffer. It was through this Mother that He became the Bridge between the Divine and the human. If we take her away, then either God does not become Man, or he that is born of her is a man, and not God. Without her we would no longer have Our Lord.

If we have a box in which we keep our money, we know the one thing we must always give attention to is the key; we never think that the key is tHe money, but we know that without the key we cannot get into our money. The Mother of the Babe is like that key; without her we cannot get to Our Lord, because He came through her. She is not to be compared to Our Lord, for she is a creature and He is the Creator. But without her we could not understand how the Bridge was built between heaven and earth.

As she formed Jesus in her body, so she forms Jesus in our souls. In this one Woman, virginity and motherhood are united, as if God willed to show that both are necessary for the world. Those things which are separated in other creatures are united in her. The Mother is the protector of the Virgin and the Virgin is also the inspiration of Motherhood.

Love Begins with a Dream

All love begins with a dream. Every person carries within his heart a blueprint of the one he loves. What seems to be love at first sight, is actually the fulfillment of a desire and the realization of a dream. We hear music for the first time and we like or dislike it, depending upon whether it harmonizes with the music that we already have in our own soul. Before we meet certain people, we already have a pattern and a mold of what we would like them to be. Some fit into it; others do not.

God too has within Himself a blueprint of everything in the universe; every flower and bird and tree and mountain and star was made according to an idea existing in His Mind. God generally has two pictures of us; one is what we are, and the other is what we ought to be. He has the model and He also has the reality, the score of the music and the way we play it.

There was one Woman in the world, however, in which there was a perfect conformity between what He wanted her to be and what she was, and that was His own Mother. He dreamed of her before she was made; He loved her before she was made. She is, even in the flesh, the ideal that God had of her. The model and the copy are perfect. She was foreseen, planned, and dreamed. The melody of her life is played just as it was written. She existed in His Divine Mind as an eternal thought. Before there were ever any mothers, she is the Mother of mothers; she is the world's first love.

New York *Sunday News* — Coloroto Magazine, Howard Christmas Tree

The Nativity (Fra Filippo Lippi and assistant), National Gallery of Art, Washington, D.C.

If You Could Choose Your Mother

Just suppose that you could have preexisted your own mother, in much the same way that an artist preexists his painting. Furthermore, suppose that you had an infinite power to make your mother anything that you pleased, just as a great artist like Raphael had the power of realizing his artistic ideals. If you had this double power, what kind of mother would you have made for yourself? Would you have made her of such a type that would make you blush because of her unwomanly and unmotherlike actions? Would you have in any way stained and soiled her with the selfishness that would make her unattractive not only to you, but to your fellowman? Would you have made her exteriorly and interiorly of such a character as to make you ashamed of her, or would you have made her, so far as human beauty goes, the most beautiful woman in the world; and so far as beauty of soul goes, one who would radiate every virtue, every manner of kindness and charity and loveliness; one who by the purity of her life and her mind and her heart would be an inspiration not only to you, but even to your fellowmen, so that all would look up to her as the very incarnation of what is best in motherhood? Now, if you who are an imperfect being and who have not the most delicate conception of all that is fine in life would have wished for the loveliest of mothers, do you think that Our Blessed Lord, Who not only preexisted His own mother, but Who had an infinite power to make her just what He chose, would, in virtue of all of the infinite delicacy of His Spirit, make her any less pure and loving and beautiful than you would have made your own mother? If you who hate selfishness would have made her selfless, and you who hate ugliness would have made her beautiful, do you not think that the Son of God Who hates sin would have made His own mother sinless, and he Who hates moral ugliness would have made her immaculately beautiful?

If you ever want to know the real qualities of a man, judge him not by his attitude to the world of commerce, his outlook on business, or his genteel manners, but judge him rather by his attitude to his own mother. If you want to know the quality of a religion, judge it exactly the same way, not by the way it seeks to please men, but rather by the attitude that it bears to the Mother of Our Blessed Lord.

Traditional

Where Love and Child Are One

History is full of the names of men who have claimed they have had a message from God. All of them without exception have appeared on the stage of history and said, "Here I am, believe me." Only one person in the world was ever preannounced; only one had His birth expected long before He came. So expected was the birth of Christ in Israel, in particular, so much did they await Him, that the teachers announced to the astrologers of the East the time and the place of His birth.

The Lord born on Christmas day is the only Person in the world who had a prehistory, a prehistory to be studied not in the slime and muck of primeval jungles, but in the bosom of the Eternal Father.

Not all children come into this world because of a distinct act of the will expressing itself in the love of man and woman. Even when the love between the two is willed, the fruit of love is conceived without their knowing it in some dark night of affection. Children are later on accepted and loved by their parents, but their decision to have a child did not necessarily beget a child, nor did their union produce an offspring.

But in the birth of Christ there was a collaboration between a woman and the Spirit of Divine Love. She willed to be a mother, and motherhood began: "Be it done unto me according to Thy will." Other mothers became conscious of motherhood through physical changes within them; Mary became conscious through spiritual change wrought by Love. And it is likely that the spiritual ecstasy that she experienced when the Holy Spirit overshadowed her was greater than ever given to man and woman in their unifying act of love.

Lovely Lady, Dressed in Blue

Lovely Lady, dressed in blue
Teach me how to pray!
God was just your little Boy
Tell me what to say!
Did you lift Him up, sometimes,
Gently on your knee?
Did you sing to Him, the way
Mother does to me?
Did you hold His hand at night?
Did you ever try
Telling stories of the world?
Oh, and did He cry?
Do you really think He cares
If I tell Him things —
Little things that happen?
And do the Angels' wings make a noise?
And can He hear me, if I speak low?
Does He understand me now?
Tell me — for you know.
Lovely Lady, dressed in blue,
Teach me how to pray.
God was just your little Boy
And you know the way.

THE MARIANIST MISSION
Mount Saint John
4435 East Patterson Road
Dayton, OH 45481-0001

Christmas: The Mother Resembles the Child

Whenever a child is born into the world, relatives speculate whether or not it resembles the father or the mother. Christmas was the first instance in history that anyone could say that the resemblance was only on the mother's side. But it is perhaps truer to say that it was not the Child who resembled the mother, but the mother who resembled the Child; for this is the Child Who made His mother. He preexisted her; she was created by Him; therefore, it was she who was the child. When the great painter Whistler was praised for the beautiful painting of his mother, he said, "You know how it is, one tries to make one's mother as nice as one can." Since Christ preexisted her, He made her beautiful as only God knows how to make a woman beautiful.

There was a further paradox in Christmas too! Mothers often tell their children when pointing to the sky, "Heaven is way up there," but when Mary held the Child in her arms, it is true to say that she looked *down* to Heaven.

Deus in adiutoriú
Domine ad adiu.
Gloria patri
Sicut erat in
principio et nunc.

God Walked Our Earth

We know too much about matter to be materialists; we know too much about the stars to think we are but stardust. A galaxy of suns and starry worlds may boast of bulk and size and speed. We too have our boast. God walked this earth!

Sometimes scientists would frighten us by reminding us of the insignificance of the earth as compared to our planetary system and the vastness of space. This bit of cosmic intimidation does not touch the heart of the problem for two reasons: man is bigger than the universe, because he can get the whole universe into his head. He is bigger than the thing he describes, different in nature from it. If he went into the suitcase he packed, he could never pack it. If he were one with atoms and suns he could never get the heavens into his head. That really leaves him only one supreme task: to get his head into the heavens. Second, our earth enjoys prominence above the rest of the universe: God walked our earth. As the poet put it:

> Not a star of all
> The innumerable hosts of stars has heard
> How He administered this terrestrial ball.
> Our race have kept their Lord's entrusted Word
>
> Of His earth-visiting peak
> None knows the secret-cherished, perilous;
> The terrible, shame-faced, frightened, whispered, sweet
> Heart shattering secret of His way with us.

The Adoration of the Magi (Joos van Gent), Metropolitan Museum of Art, Bequest of George Blumenthal, 1941

Christmas: First Note in a New Symphony

Imagine the conductor of a symphony giving to each member of the orchestra a well-scored composition. Each of the musicians is free to follow the notes to produce orchestral harmony. But suppose one of them deliberately strikes a sour note. In the face of it, the director may do one of two things: he may strike his baton and order them to play it over, or he may ignore the discord. It makes little difference which he does, for that false note is traveling out in space at about a thousand feet a second; and as long as time endures there will always be found a discord in the universe.

Is there any way to restore harmony to the world? It could be done only by someone reaching out his hand from eternity and stopping that unhappy note in its mad flight. But would it still not be a false note, even though it could go no further? It would cease being a discord if he who stopped it wrote a new symphony and made that false note the first note in the new melody. Then it would be harmonious.

Centuries ago God gave to man a symphony of creation and with it the glorious gift of freedom. Man chose to introduce a discord into the universe by the abuse of freedom, by choosing a part to the whole, a fruit for the garden, and his rebellion became a kind of infection which passed on to every human being.

God could have ignored this infected humanity. Rather what He did was to ask a woman to give Him a human nature—one that would not have this stain of rebellion and dissent. Dispensing with the carnal union of man and woman, His human nature broke that bond with awful humanity. It was a kind of a lock in the canal of human generation, by which one passed from foul water to clear water. This human nature, conceived and born of a virgin, became the first note in a new creation or a regenerated humanity.

The human race, therefore, is divided into two classes of people: the "once born," who are begotten of the flesh; and the "twice born," who are begotten also of the Spirit in Christ. Every human being who incorporates himself to Christ becomes like a new note in this symphony of the "New Humanity," and the sum of all is what Scripture calls the Mystical "Body of Christ" or the Church. This is true humanism.

His Name Shall Be JESUS

The Name of Jesus is not found in the Old Testament, because the Old Testament was written in Hebrew, and Jesus is a Greek name. But it is found in the New Testament, which was written in Greek. A name in one language is not the same as in another. For example, the name John in German is Hans and in Russian, Ivan, and in Italian, Giovanni. If the Child were given a Hebrew name instead of a Greek name, He would have been called Joshua, Jesus being the Greek for the Hebrew Joshua.

The Divine Child was named after Joshua, the commander in chief of the Lord's people, under whom they conquered their inheritance. He was the one who brought them out of the desert to the land flowing with milk and honey; he was the one who led them to victory, though the foes were strong and crafty.

But when this Old Testament Joshua, or Jesus, died, a time came when the people had lost their land and were carried away again into captivity. Then a second Jesus appears, as Joshua now becomes *Jeshua,* the high priest, who led the people back to the land that had been lost through their infidelity. It was he who rebuilt the temple, restored the worship of God, and was said by the prophet Zachariah to be the forerunner of the great High Priest Who was to come.

The angel told Joseph that "Mary has conceived through the Holy Spirit and she will give birth to a Son, Whom you will call Jesus (the Savior) for it is He Who will save the people from their sins." Because He is a spiritual Savior, rather than a political or economic savior, the promise of the Child as Savior was given to Joseph, who had a deeper experience of sin than did the Mother Mary. On the other hand, Mary, who is characterized by promptness of personal devotion, is given the promise of *Christ* as King (Luke 1:32,33). Joshua then was an immanent type of Our Lord, Who is the Captain of our salvation, Who fought out the fearful conflict for us against the deadly enemy of sin, Who leads His people through the river of death unto everlasting life. Joshua led the children of Israel into Cana as Jesus leads His people into Heaven.

54

eis in adiutoriu
meum intende.
Domine ad
adiuuandum

me festina .

New York *Sunday News* — Coloroto Magazine

The Divine Infection

Most of the infections which we know are bad infections, but Christmas was the beginning of a good infection, for it made possible for us, who are mere sons of our parents, to become sons of God.

C. S. Lewis in his work *Mere Christianity* uses the example of toy soldiers to explain Christmas. He asks if a boy does not often think what fun it would be if a tin soldier were turned into flesh and blood. In the Incarnation we have one human being out of all humanity who did become completely Divinized, but as Lewis goes on to point out, the illustration breaks down here. If one tin soldier came to life, it would make no difference to the rest of the tin soldiers. They are all separate. But human beings are not: "If you could see humanity spread out in time as God sees it, it would not look like a lot of separate things dotted about. It would look like one single growing thing — rather like a very complicated tree. Every individual would appear connected with every other individual — consequently when Christ becomes man, it is not really as if you could become one particular tin soldier. It is as if something which is always affecting the human mass begins at one point to affect the whole human mass in a new way. From that point on, the effect spreads through all mankind." Humanity is already "saved in principle," but since that first Christmas, individuals have to appropriate that salvation by considerable effort; namely, by making ourselves disposable to the Divine infection. And if we get close enough to Him, we catch it. And that is how we get over being humanly sick.

How to Find Christmas Peace

How to find Christmas peace in a world of unrest? You cannot find peace on the *outside*, but you can find peace on the inside by letting God do to your soul what Mary let Him do to her body, namely, let Christ be formed in you. As she cooked the meals in her Nazarene home, as she nursed her aged cousin, as she drew water at the well, as she prepared the meals of the village carpenter, as she knitted the seamless garment, as she kneaded the dough and swept the floor, she was conscious that Christ was in her; that she was a living Ciborium, a monstrance of the Divine Eucharist, a Gate of Heaven through which a Creator would peer upon creation, a Tower of Ivory up whose chaste body He was to climb "to kiss upon her lips a mystic rose."

As He was physically formed in her, so He wills to be spiritually formed in you. If you knew He was seeing through your eyes, you would see in every fellowman a child of God. If you knew that He worked through your hands, they would bless all the day through. If you knew He spoke through your lips, then your speech, like Peter's, would betray that you had been with the Galilean. If you knew that He wants to use your mind, your will, your fingers, and your heart, how different you would be. If half the world did this, there would be no war!

Rouen Cathedral (Claude Monet), Metropolitan Museum of Art, Bequest of Theodore M. Davis, 1915

Restoration
by the Divine Artist

If you know that you could be better than you are; if you feel like the master painting of a great artist that has become somewhat defaced and stained; if you know that though you are too good for the rubbish heap, you are nevertheless too spoiled to hang in the Metropolitan Museum; if you know that you cannot restore yourself to your pristine beauty; if you know that no one could restore you better than the Divine Artist who made you—then you have already taken the first step toward peace. The Divine Artist did come to restore the original and He came on Christmas Day. Such is the meaning of Christmas. The Son of God became man that man might become the adopted son of God.

It's Free

Christmas starts with the fact than man cannot lift himself by his own bootstraps. His own intelligence is too limited to understand higher truths; his own will is too weak to carry through all his resolves, even when he knows what is truth. So God came down to this world to take human nature and make it the model and pattern of how our natures are to be lifted up to His.

If the chemicals, plants, and animals of the world are ever to be part of our kingdom or our nature which thinks, scans the universe, loves, knows the secrets of the stars, it is necessary that man go down to them and lift them up into his own nature. So too before man can ever live a truly Divine Life, God must come down to him, for man cannot make himself partake of Divine Life any more than oxygen can make itself a violet.

Unlike the plants, chemicals, and the animals, however, who are not consulted before being taken up to our human life, God will not violate the freedom which He gave man. Hence, the human Nature which He took to Himself in Bethlehem was assumed because of the free surrender of a Woman. So too with us, there is no violent seizure of our will; we must give ourselves freely and completely. This involves a dying to our lower nature, which some refuse to do.

Once this Christmas spirit seizes a soul, it transforms it. Christmas is thus perpetuated and becomes a living thing called Christianity, as we freely give our wills to His Will to be strengthened, our minds to His Intellect to know Truth, and our flesh to His Flesh to be purified. It is all free, but we are so frightened that if we give our finger to the Babe He will seize our hand. But what peace to be ravished by Love!

New York *Sunday News* — Coloroto Magazine, Air Force Chapel, Colorado Springs, Colo.

Where Is He That Is Born "King"?

Head of The Good Thief (Domenico Beccafumi), Pierpont Morgan Library Collection

We Americans are very fond of our democracy. We boast of our equality and we give a little extra homage to the "underdog." But at the same time, there is a hidden desire for royalty and nobility. Though we have no kings on thrones, we have such monarchs as "Asparagus King," "Movie Queen," and "Hot Dog King," and we crown Miss America.

Man is always seeking for a king, because he feels in the depths of his being that he is never so great as when he is in the presence of the greater. Once a great man appears, the smaller fish rally as parasites to the whale. Communism no longer calls anyone "Comrade." They have jumped through the bourgeoisie to a love of royalty.

How do we account for this instinct in the human race to make ourselves exalted by bowing to another? This desire for kingship is a craving deeply implanted in our nature by the Creator. That is why in the Christmas story we find the question, "Where is He that is born King?" Distracted hearts settle for tinsel-crowned kings, but they are actually in search of a King of Kings in Whom the human heart at last finds its true rest. This title of King was not used of Our Lord again until the Passion, when it fell from the lips of the pagan Pilate. The charge laid against Jesus was that He had acted as a King and therefore was a rival to Caesar. The truth is that when the people attempted to make Him a bread King, He withdrew from them and went into the mountains alone. Before Pilate He did not deny His Kingly character, but only affirmed, "My Kingdom is not of this world." The title on the Cross was not radically untrue. He was a King. The penitent robber came close to the truth when he said, "Remember me, when Thou cometh into Thy Kingdom." It was borne into his mind that in some mysterious way the kingdom was to be reached through the Cross and lay beyond it. Herod was afraid that the Divine Child might become an earthly King. But as we sing in one of the Christmas Hymns, "He takes away no earthly crowns Who gives heavenly ones." The world wants a King, but the true King is One Who rules in the mind, sways hearts, and conquers sin. That was why the Apostles were commissioned to make known "another King, one Jesus" (Acts 17:7).

Depose

Peace on Earth

To the descendants of the shepherds and the wise men, to the souls which still have roots, to all men of good will, whether they be Jew, Protestant, or Catholic, atheists, pagans, or enemies, the plea goes out to seek the Truth even though it be found in a place you presently believe to be as repugnant as a stable. That Babe came to earth at a time when the social order was most ripe for class war. There was conflict between Jew and Gentile; Samaritan and Jew; Roman and Greek; Scribe and Pharisee; "haves and have-nots"; dictators and oppressed; Caesars and anti-Caesars, and yet instead of capitalizing on any one class to win support, He chose the hard way—by preaching the unity of all men, first in Adam, then regenerated in Him, living in concord and peace through the charity of His Holy Spirit.

The Son of God,
Our Brother Man

We read in the Gospel, "The Word became Flesh," but we do not read, "God became a concept." About sixty times in the Gospels Our Lord refers to Himself as "The Son of Man"; that is, humanity. There is no agony, distress, fear, hunger, thirst, trial, suffering which man can experience that this Child in the crib did not come to pass through. He is the Brother Man to the sick neighbor, to the crazy mixed-up teenager who wants to be herself and yet slavishly follows her sister slaves, to the prisoner in agony, paying for his crime in prison, to the "rock and roller" with his long hair, to the joy-starved butterfly of a girl pretending she is having a good time, and to the existentialists, the atheists, the mockers. There is not a person in the world who does not feel within himself the triple rebellion which was passed on to us through the rebellion of humanity when it began, namely, lust, or the war of the erotic against the reasonable; pride, or the exaltation of the ego with its contempt of neighbor; or finally, greed, or the inordinate tendency to make character identical with *having* rather than with *being*.

Now can it be that the repercussions of the first sin are greater in humanity than the repercussions of the Incarnation? Shall the first Adam exercise a greater impact on us than the second Adam? If we have Adam in us as our head in the natural order, is not every man—Buddhist, Communist, atheist—a sharer in some way of our Head in the Divine order? Why do so many treat Him as a brother-in-law instead of as a Brother?

There is a distance of over thirty years that separates the shepherds crying "Behold, the Child" and Pilate shouting "Behold, the Man," but it is the same Person—God Who became Man and was not ashamed to be the Brother of us poor mortals.

(Luca della Robbia), National Gallery of Art, Washington, D.C., Samuel H. Kress Collection

Why We Give Gifts at Christmas

The best way to understand the feast of Christmas is in terms of a gift. We spend 364 days in getting; Christmas we spend in giving. The greater part of the year, we inflate our ego and insist on our rights; on Christmas day, we deflate our ego to bring happiness to others. It is the one day of the year we have "enlargement of the heart."

The reason we give on Christmas day is because we too have received a Gift—the Gift of God to man, in which He humbled Himself so completely as to veil His Glory and His Power. The Divine Babe did not come into the world as one would walk into a museum to see the work of other artists; He came into the world as a painter into His own studio. His entrance was into the world that He had made.

As the veil of the temple of Jerusalem hid the glory of God, so the human flesh veiled His Glory or Shekinah. God became man and gave us the gift of Himself, and in so doing, He experienced cold, hunger, thirst, weariness, exile, torture, and suffering of the most intense kind. Never again could man say, "God does not know what it is to suffer." Never again could man say that in offering his life for a friend, he could make a nobler sacrifice than God; for Our Lord came to offer His Life for humanity. This is His great gift to us, and therefore we give gifts on Christmas because we received a Gift. It is the birthday of God in the form of man, in order that man might be like unto God. Whenever we give gifts, we tear off the price tag so that there will be no proportion between the gift of the lover and the love of the giver. There is no price tag on the Gift of Christ. We can never buy Him, but we can sell Him, as Judas did. His Gift of Love is free—is that why we scorn it?

Winter on the Farm, Transparency by Francis G. Mayer, N.Y.C.

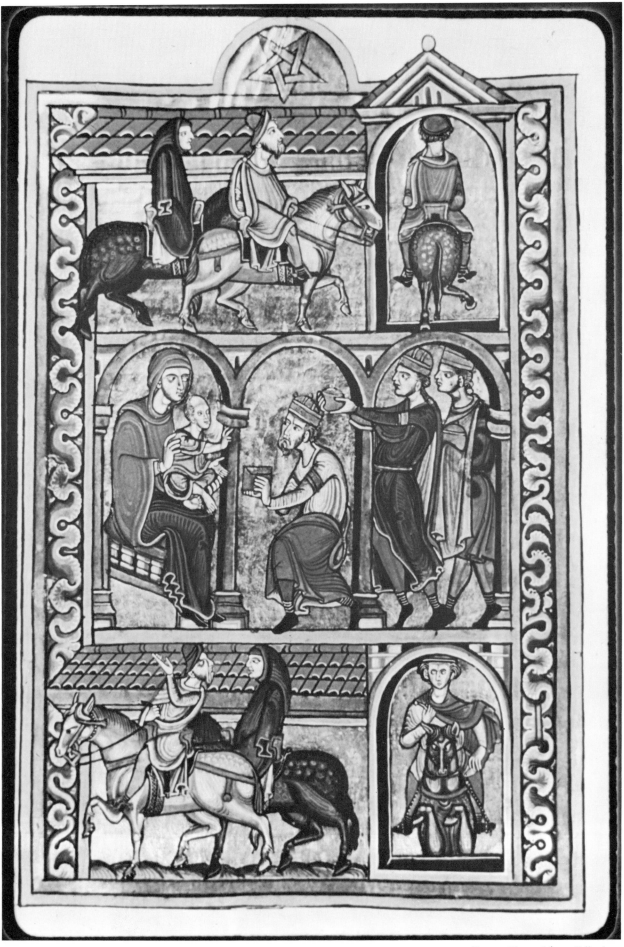

How Would You Like to Be a Snake?

It is hard for us to understand the humility involved in the Word becoming flesh, or God becoming man. Imagine, if it were possible, a human person divesting himself of his body, and then sending his soul into the body of a serpent. A double humiliation would follow; first, accepting the limitation of a serpentine organism, knowing all the while his mind was superior, and that fangs could not adequately articulate thoughts no serpent ever possessed. The second humiliation would be to be forced as a result of this "emptying of self" to live in the companionship of servants.

But all this is nothing compared to the emptying of God, by which He took on the form of man and accepted the limitations of a human nature, such as hunger and persecution. Not trivial either was it for the Wisdom of God to condemn Himself to association with poor fishermen who knew so little. He Who is the Word now has to use words, and to live with stupid men and weak mortals. This humiliation, which began in Bethlehem when He was first conceived in the Virgin Mary, was only the first of many to counteract the pride of man, until the final humiliation of death on the Cross.

If there were no Cross, there would have been no Crib; if there had been no nails, there would have been no straw. But He could not *teach* the lesson of the Cross as payment for sin; He had to *take* it. God the Father did not spare His Son—so much did He love mankind. That was the secret wrapped in the swaddling bands. If you would find it hard to be a snake and live with snakes, how do you think it feels for God to become a man and live with men.

Je vous salue, Marie!, Old print

Adoration of the Shepherds (Andrea Mantegna), Metropolitan Museum of Art, Anonymous Gift, 1932

Emile Breton

Traditional

Old prints

The Cradle and the Cross

She gave birth to her first child, a son. And as there was no place for them inside the inn, she wrapped him up and laid him in a manger.

(Luke 2:7)

And when they came to the place called the Skull, they crucified him with the criminals.

(Luke 23:33)

Is it easier to understand the love of the cross than the love of the cradle, the love that manifests itself in giving up life for another than the love which humbles itself in infancy that men might never boast of their greatness?

He accepted the manger because there was no room in the inn; He accepted the cross because men said, "We will not have this Man reign over us." Disowned upon entering His own creation, He is rejected upon leaving it. He was laid in a stranger's stable at the beginning of life and a stranger's grave at the end. At His crib in Bethlehem, He was flanked by an ox and an ass, and on the cross of Calvary by two thieves. Swaddling clothes bound Him in His birthplace; swaddling clothes wrapped Him in His tomb.

His Life was lived not just from Bethlehem to Calvary, rather it began with Calvary. The Cross was there at the beginning. It cast its shadow backward to His Birth. We ordinary mortals go from the known to the unknown, submitting ourselves to forces beyond our control. That is why the life of so many of us is a tragedy. But He went from the known to the known, from the reason for His coming, namely to be Jesus, or Savior, to the fulfillment of His coming, namely, the death on the Cross.

Hence, there was no tragedy in His Life, for tragedy implies the unforeseeable, the uncontrollable, the fatalistic. Modern life is tragic when there is spiritual darkness and unredeemable guilt. For the Christ Child there were no uncontrollable forces, no submission to fatalistic change from which there could be no escape; but there was an "inscape"—the microcosmic manger summarizing the macrocosmic cross on Calvary.

For all the people who know themselves to be stables, inhabited by inner beasts, and who give Him welcome, there is a joy that makes them shout in their hearts—"Merry Christmas, Merry Christmas."

Merry Christmas

I want you to have a Merry Christmas, but I know you cannot be merry without a reason, and the only reason there is a Christmas is because there is a Christ! I want you to have a feast, but you cannot have a feast without a festival, and this is the Birthday of the Savior. I want you to have peace, but you cannot have peace without a Peacemaker. I want you to be merry, but you cannot be merry without attending a wedding: the nuptials of God and man in the unity of the Person of the Son of God.